D0566116

Love FROM Grandma

TO

FROM

DATE

Love from Grandma

Revised and Edited

Copyright © 1995, 1998 Becky L. Amble

Published by Front Porch Books, a division of Garborg's, LLC
P.O. Box 20132
Bloomington, MN 55420

Design by Jennifer Parker

All rights reserved. No part of this book
may be reproduced in any form without
permission in writing from the publisher.

ISBN 1-58375-422-9

Dedication

To Grandma Betsey

Acknowledgments

All the grandmothers

Norman Vincent Peale and Sybil Light of
the Peale Center for Christian Living

A special thank you to Tessie for her diligent help,
and to Dave and Louise for the hours of encouragement.

Thank you to all of the people who passed out my questionnaires,
and especially to all of the women who took the time to write
their advice. I wish we could have used everyone's material.

All of the grandmothers have given me permission to use
their first name, initial of their last name, age, and
either home town or current residence.

INTRODUCTION

I believe God made grandmothers different from everyone else. They seem to love unconditionally—just as God does—holding us close to their hearts, wanting to protect and guide us. If we will only take the time to look and listen, they are always there for us.

My own Grandma Betsey was a special person in my life—the only living grandparent I knew. My best memories are of sitting with her. We never had to do anything special—just be together.

The idea for this book developed out of my own workplace trend research as I noted high levels of stress and uncertainty among Americans at every age. After sending out over 200 questionnaires to grandmothers throughout America seeking messages they would like to share to help their grandchildren live a fulfilling life, this project took on a life of its own.

Love, From Grandma is more than a book of advice, it is a book of love. Maybe your grandmother is in this book, or maybe she is speaking through one of these grandmothers.

Becky L. Amble is an accomplished businesswoman, marketer, and researcher. She has been cited as a trend-spotter by The Wall Street Journal and USA Today. She works at the Minneapolis StarTribune as a group leader and marketing manager in the rentals market group. She is also involved with several professional, civic, and community groups.

Becky grew up in North Dakota and now lives with her husband, Marshall Gravdahl, their son, Alex, and two cats, AlleyCat and Greta, in Woodbury, Minnesota.

FOREWORD

Our grandmothers often define the very best in us. Childhood memories of lessons learned at her knee become lessons to be followed in adulthood. The grandmother's position is an enviable one; all the good parts of listening and loving, playing and reading, praising and spoiling without the daily routine and problem solving. Her role allows nurturing and coaxing. From the vaulted position of grandmother, she can speak volumes about what's good and right and honest and pure. A grandmother can instill values and morals and truth through her wisdom and warmth.

NORMAN VINCENT PEALE

Pawling, New York

What is a Grandma?

The following was written by a third grader for a school assignment:

A grandma is a lady who has no children of her own, so she likes other people's little girls. Grandmas don't have anything to do except be here. They are so old they should not play hard. It is enough if they drive us to the supermarket where the pretend horse is and have lots of dimes ready, or if they take us for walks they should slow down past pretty things like leaves and caterpillars. Usually they are fat, but not too fat. They wear glasses and funny underwear. They can take their teeth and gums off. They don't have to be smart, only answer questions like why dogs hate cats and how come God isn't married. When they read to us they don't skip words or mind if it is the same story again. Everybody should try to have a grandma, especially if they don't have a television, because grandmas are the only grownups who have got time.

Thank you to Grandmother Patricia B.
of Palmer, Alaska for sending this to us.

Take care of yourself. Love, Grandma

Life is a superb gift from God; treasure it!
Make the most of every day and every opportunity.
Each day is precious and filled with promise.

HARRIET B., 73, LAKE PARK, MINNESOTA

Your future lies in your hands. Earn respect for who you are and what you stand for. Be strong about your beliefs and what you want to accomplish in life.

JANE W., 59, MINNEAPOLIS, MINNESOTA

Learn how to give and take in order to live as peacefully as you can. Peace within is the best happiness we can achieve.

LEONA H., 72, BILLINGS, MONTANA

Always remember that you are unique; there is no one else like you. You are a child of a loving God and have inherent and infinite worth. Understanding that enables you to fulfill your unique potential, a condition for abundant living.

CHRISTINA S., 76, SPOKANE, WASHINGTON

Life is like a play: you have the leading role. Make it an Oscar performance.

KATHIE J., 50, LITTLE CANADA, MINNESOTA

A positive attitude will help you through difficult times and make life better for you and others. The way you live your life can make a difference; caring and kindness are contagious. God made you unique and special and He loves you no matter what.

EILEEN J., 62, RED WING, MINNESOTA

Only you can determine what kind of life you will lead, so make it meaningful. You have this one life; fill it with all the joy and happiness you can.

HELEN B., 84, ROSEVILLE, MINNESOTA

Love other people as brothers and sisters. Be kind, courteous, and supportive. Meditate frequently on the Word of God and look to Him for strength and guidance.

ROXANN M., 55, MOUNDS VIEW, MINNESOTA

Life is short and involves hard work, so make it count for something. Remember that no matter what you do, it always affects someone else. Be ready not only to accept congratulations, but also responsibility. Use your mistakes as an opportunity to learn.

JEANETTE S., 57, MONTEREY, CALIFORNIA

Find your greatest contentment in your own company. Don't postpone the great adventure of reading biographies, history, short stories, and essays.

MARY G., 65, OMAHA, NEBRASKA

Be curious and continue to learn new things as long as you are able.

NELL S., 58, NEWMAN GROVE, NEBRASKA

Just be yourself; it's the way God made you and it's very fulfilling. Learn self-control and you will become a strong, genuinely independent person. Don't act on impulse, but think things through.

IRENE S., 57, ROTHSAY, MINNESOTA

Life is not always a bed of roses. Learn to accept the disappointments or things you cannot change, but stand tall and be proud of who you are.

WILMA H., 70, TULARE, SOUTH DAKOTA

Do not pass up interesting opportunities. Learn from experience. Do not be afraid to take chances. Life is a challenge; roll with the punches, take a deep breath, and try again.

MARYONA J., 72, MILES CITY, MICHIGAN

Remember that character, dignity, and dependability are vital in life. Face your problems squarely; don't leave them for another day or for someone else to solve for you. Live each day as though it were your last, because some opportunities will not come your way again.

NORMA T., 85, RENO, NEVADA

Experience your uniqueness. There is no one else on earth who has your combination of qualities. No one else on earth can make your observations or give your insights.

VIVIAN L., 73, MORA, MINNESOTA

Learn to laugh at your minor mistakes and to learn from the earth-shaking ones.

SHARON K., 50, CHICAGO, ILLINOIS

Live your life as if everything you do will be on the front page of the newspaper. Have faith, and love your fellow man. Be determined and set examples for your own children. Show kindness to all.

LETA C., 70, MIDLAND, MICHIGAN

To "love your neighbor as yourself" starts by loving yourself and multiplies by sharing that love with others. Unconditional love brings a joyous energy that will surely bless your life with peace.

LOIS V., 54, CLEAR LAKE, WISCONSIN

When you are tempted to follow the crowd, believe in yourself. Don't be afraid to be different. Everyone admires an individual who has principles.

DODIE P., 62, OTTAWA, CANADA

You will get out of life what you put into it. I have several "rules for life": Accentuate the positive. Do what comes naturally. Remember your roots. It's good to improve yourself, but never think that you are better than anyone else. Keep it simple. The simple things in life are best!

KARLENE S., 59, HOLYOKE, MASSACHUSETTS

Reflect on your life. Reflect also on God. Knowledge of God is not passive. Read, listen, and reflect. Align yourself with others who do this.

BETTY M., 65, ROCHESTER, MINNESOTA

Everything you do, think, or say is very important. It does not matter what other people think. You know who you are and you are very special. God loves you and I love you.

PAT D., 57, MISSION, TEXAS

Set short-term goals first with long-term expectations. Don't be disappointed if you have to make adjustments. Life is full of adjustments and you have to learn to be flexible.

BONNIE P., 54, SEATTLE, WASHINGTON

Take care of your family and friends. Love, Grandma

Keep family ties strong. You need your independence, but a close family circle can help you through the tough times and give you great joy.

JUDY F., 59, WOLCOTT, INDIANA

Actions really do speak louder than words. I believe that children are a reflection of their parents, and grandchildren are the blessings, the reward of a job well done. We all need someone to follow, someone to look up to; that's the privilege of being a grandmother.

GLORIA W., 69, FRANKLIN LAKES, NEW JERSEY

Family and friends should be very important to you in your everyday life.

JEAN K., 70, FORT DODGE, IOWA

Be grateful to your parents; raising a child is not an easy task.

ALEXIA L., 64, CLEVELAND, OHIO

"Riches" does not mean money alone. Family, friendships, and health are riches to be desired more than money.

SHIRLEY R., 70, DAYTON, OHIO

When dating, always question whether you could be proud, happy, loving, and secure sharing life with that potential spouse. Looks and popularity are not the most important. Love, sincerity, and commitment are! Be selective, but realistic.

JAN A., 59, PRESCOTT, ARIZONA

Don't prepare so much for your wedding that you lose sight of the marriage.

BARBARA M., 65, MOUND, MINNESOTA

Choose a lifetime partner whose family background, values, and goals are similar to yours. The same sort of church background is very helpful. If you differ, discuss your differences and their importance to you before marriage. Be prepared for disagreements and try to resolve them; don't run away at the first obstacle. Living together before marriage is not a commitment, but a "cop-out" which does not necessarily lead to a long, happy marriage.

MARTHA B., 72, CHARLOTTE, MICHIGAN

Your family loves you, so keep close to them through letters, telephone calls, and visits.

LILLIAN J., 78, GRAND FORKS, NORTH DAKOTA

Always try to communicate with your parents; they are smarter than you think.

MARGE D., 58, REYNOLDS, INDIANA

Treat your parents with respect and don't forget to be proud of where you came from.

LaVonne H., 62, Moorhead, Minnesota

Say "I love you" to those you do love.

Beatrice W., 62, Coon Rapids, Minnesota

Value your family and friends, and call your grandmother once a week!

CHARLOTTE D., 60,
DAYTON, OHIO

Let your children know you love them. Spoil and enjoy them from infancy to adulthood. But be firm with discipline and explain why if necessary. Always praise their efforts, no matter how minor. And keep their imaginations alive. Children love to hear stories of the old days.

ELIZABETH T., 70,
ST. CLAIR SHORES, MICHIGAN

Take care of others. Love, Grandma

Be loving and caring with people, for we are God's children. Care for His creation and the gifts we have been given; they are ours to borrow and pass on to others in better condition than we found them in if possible.

CAROLYN C., 62, CRYSTAL, MINNESOTA

Enjoy all the gifts of life: nature, the arts, literature, food. But most of all enjoy the people—family, friends, community, and the chance acquaintance. Listen, listen to what they say, respect their thoughts, think upon them.

Jo G., 57, Red Lodge, Montana

Be quick to say "I'm sorry" when you are to blame, and mean it! Be slow to judge others, for as you judge, so you will be judged. Be honest in all your dealings.

AGNES B., 85, SAN JOSE, CALIFORNIA

Don't always think about yourself. What you give, in return will make you feel much happier.

SHIRLEY P., 71, ROSEVILLE, MINNESOTA

Keep in contact with friends and family; know that they are there to support you in any way that you need. Make new friends, too, to enrich and broaden your life.

CAROL P., 57, HARRISVILLE, RHODE ISLAND

Be giving and forgiving. Seek out the good in people and love unconditionally. Be in control of your life, but don't try to control others.

PENNY B., 55, IRVING, TEXAS

Accept, encourage, and support how different we all are.

JUDY A., 57, BALDWIN, NEW YORK

Be loyal to your friends and keep a sense of humor. It helps with life's downs. Don't let silly misunderstandings cause major problems with friends or fellow workers. Be kind and try to see both sides of a problem. Above all, my dear grandchild, know that you are loved, and keep in touch.

DOROTHY G., 71, NORTHVILLE, MICHIGAN

Never go against your good judgment to follow a peer or group in the wrong direction. Be strong, do right, and enjoy a successful life. Be considerate of others, especially the less fortunate.

THESTINA T., 84, GRAND FORKS, NORTH DAKOTA

Do not let unkind thoughts become unkind words.

PATRICIA B., 56, PALMER, ALASKA

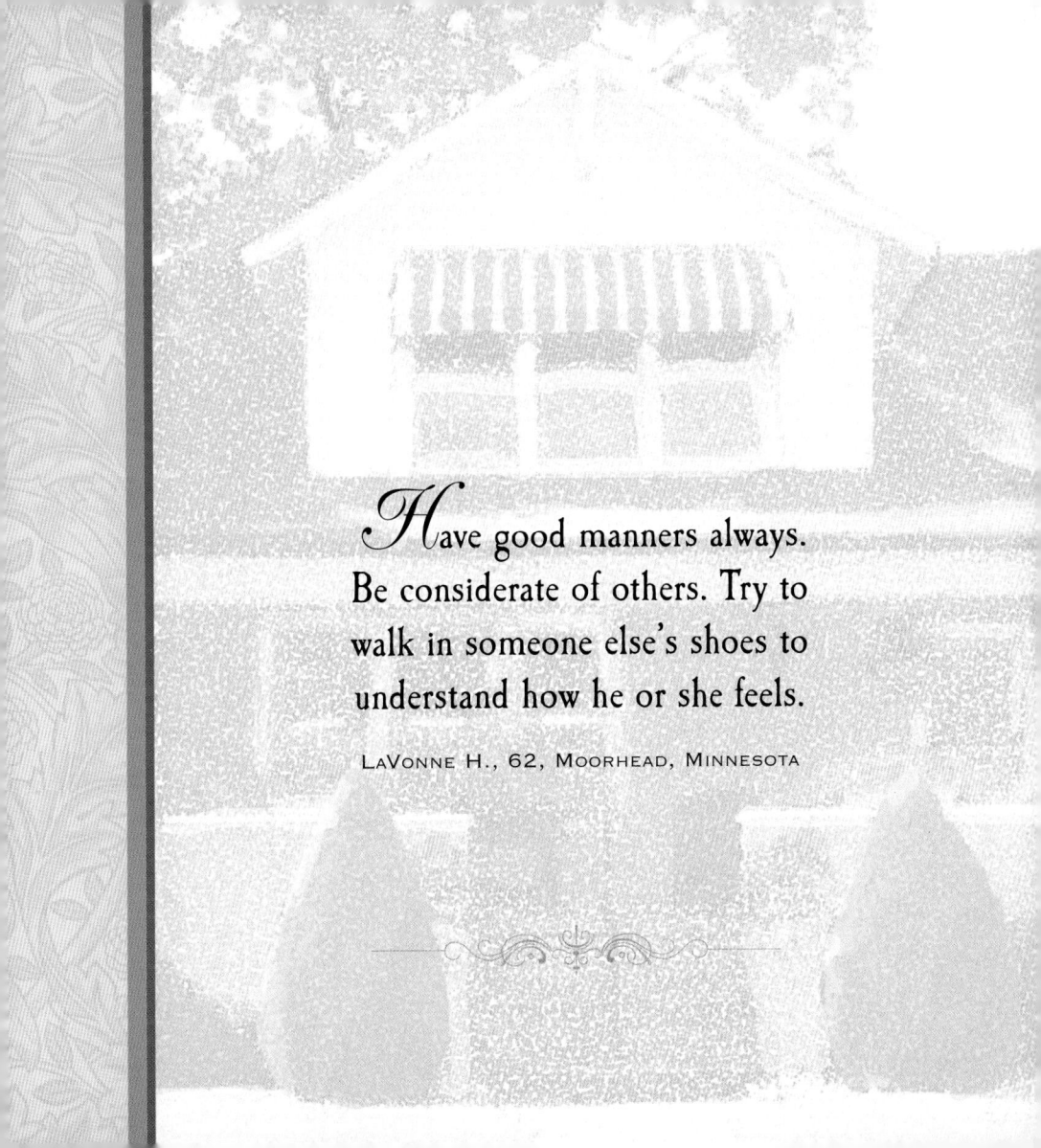

Have good manners always. Be considerate of others. Try to walk in someone else's shoes to understand how he or she feels.

LaVonne H., 62, Moorhead, Minnesota

Be kind
to everyone,
especially
older people.

DOROTHY H., 83,
BEMIDJI, MINNESOTA

Live your life with a positive attitude
and surround yourself with positive people.
Treat everyone you meet, young or old,
with kindness and an open mind.

EDITH G., 65, METHUEN, MASSACHUSETTS

Have compassion instead of rebellion,
understanding instead of judgment,
and above all, have love and caring.
Always remember to respect people
for themselves and not for what
they can do for you.

ELIZABETH S., 71, KAMUELA, HAWAII

Manners are very important and will help you throughout your life. A smile and a friendly manner plus a genuine "thank you" can save the day!

IDA K., 70, ST. PAUL, MINNESOTA

Fill yourself with love, grace, warmth, and sensitivity. Do something for someone else every day of your life, preferably anonymously. Remember, God wants us to love others.

GRACIE G., 68, ALPENA, MICHIGAN

Think before you speak. Saving a friendship is more important than saving face. Enjoy yourself, but never at someone else's expense. All people are God's children. We are in a diverse and interesting world.

DODIE P., 62, OTTAWA, ONTARIO, CANADA

Always be honest and open. Have good communication with others. Treat all people with respect regardless of race or income.

IRENE H., 70, AVON, MINNESOTA

To have a friend, you must be one. Friends of all ages make life interesting. Laugh and have fun. Do something to help others. There are so many good causes and so few volunteers.

LILLIAN J., 78, GRAND FORKS, NORTH DAKOTA

Get to know people of many races, religions, and cultures, and learn to appreciate their uniqueness. Share your ideas, dreams, time, talents, and material goods. Develop your ability to be a friend, to be caring and supportive. Above all, give God the glory in all good things that come your way.

MAE LOU T., 60, BERESFORD, SOUTH DAKOTA

Show love, patience, and compassion. It is in giving, not getting, that our lives are blessed. Remember that a life worth living is filled with giving and forgiving.

RUTH R., 88, FORT DODGE, IOWA

Learn from the mistakes and experiences of others as well as from your own.

MARY D., 54, PEORIA, ILLINOIS

Work hard and apply yourself, but don't forget to enjoy life and your relationships. Try to see something positive in each and every person you come in contact with. Make friends with people from all walks of life and you will be a terrific adult.

DOROTHY B., 59, ST. PAUL, MINNESOTA

Regardless of how others treat you, think of how you would like to be treated and follow that path.

ETHEL S., 75,
WOODBURY, CONNECTICUT

Trust your instincts; trust your judgment. Never be cruel. Love all the creatures of the world. Love others. Love yourself.

LEE C., 75, MUNICH, GERMANY

Take care of your spirit. Love, Grandma

Develop a strong spiritual life. It will ease the problems and difficulties of life and enhance its joys and successes.

JO G., 57, RED LODGE, MONTANA

The best advice I can give is to have faith, hope, and charity. Have faith in God, a personal relationship with our living Savior, and faith in yourself. Have hope for the future and take a positive approach to everything. And have charity to share yourself and your talents with others and to give help to those who are in need.

OLIVE B., 62, HATTON, NORTH DAKOTA

Live life each day fully for God. Greet each morning with the prayer, "Lord, what are You and I going to do together today? I'm reporting for duty."
You'll never be bored.

PEARL S., 62, HOUSTON, TEXAS

Prayer changes things. Trust in the Lord.

RUTH R., 88, FORT DODGE, IOWA

When you were born you became a gift to your family. You are a special child of God.

ELLA B., 62, TRONDHEIM, NORWAY

Love God, then love and care for yourself, your family, and others—in this order. If you truly love God and yourself, everything else will fall into place.

KATHY P., 56, NEW MARKET, ALABAMA

Nurture your spiritual health even more than your physical health. Seek God, love God, love yourself; then you can love others. Believe in the triumph of good always. Express gratitude to your family, friends, associates, and God.

BECKY ANN S., 74, WEST LAFAYETTE, INDIANA

If you start your day with prayer, God will lead and guide you. Remember, God is on call twenty-four hours a day.

ARLEEN K., 71, THOMPSON, NORTH DAKOTA

Always carry God's love with you. It will enable you to understand and to forgive.

RUTH C., 77, SIOUX FALLS, SOUTH DAKOTA

Take time to be quiet and talk to God. Enjoy the beauty of creation and preserve it. Above all, give God the glory in all good things that come your way.

MAE LOU T., 60, BERESFORD, SOUTH DAKOTA

You are a child of a loving God and have inherent and infinite worth.

CHRISTINA S., 76, SPOKANE, WASHINGTON

Everyone you meet is made in God's image. Give them the respect and the dignity they deserve as His children.

SANDY L., 47, PLYMOUTH, MINNESOTA

Stay close to the Lord; He'll give you guidance and wisdom. You have to take time to receive it. If you do there will be no challenge in your life that His counsel cannot help you to solve.

HELEN B., 72, MINNEAPOLIS, MINNESOTA

Treasure honesty, both in listening to
the Spirit within and in dealing with all people.
Build a strong and personal relationship with God.
Do all you can to deepen that bond of love and
trust between the Creator and yourself.

MARIANNE W., 64, ST. PAUL, MINNESOTA

Always take joy in the little things God gives you, along with His greater gifts. Don't keep your relationship with God too sacred. Talk to Him when you're in the shower or stuck in traffic.

JUDY R., 48, BRECKENRIDGE, MINNESOTA

Become acquainted with God. Talk to Him as you walk, dream, or pray. He listens.

ALLEGRA V., 71, MIDLAND, MICHIGAN

Go to church and find friends there.
Try to find a good community to live in.
Start out, if possible, in a place where
you have friends and relatives.

MARION M., 75, CANBY, OREGON

Always think of yourself as loved by God, who is Love.

MARGARET MARY M., 70, MORRIS, MINNESOTA

Attend Sunday School and church. Believe in God. He will keep you on the right path and help you through all your trials.

BEATRICE W., 62, COON RAPIDS, MINNESOTA

Life in all forms is a gift from God. If life seems too complicated, return to your childhood faith. You will see the right path to take.

MURIEL O., 68, THOMPSON, NORTH DAKOTA

If you make mistakes, ask God to forgive you and accept that you are forgiven. Put a high value on yourself. You are what God made you to be.

IRENE S., 57, ROTHSAY, MINNESOTA

Have an abiding faith in our loving God who created all things. Choose Jesus, the way of love, and you choose abundant, eternal life.

MARJ C., 74, ATWOOD, KANSAS

Say your prayers every day. Strong faith in God can pull you through the darkest of times.

PATRICIA B., 56, PALMER, ALASKA

Walk with God. Life is difficult and He has much to teach as you walk through, and grow because of, those hard times.

GERRY L., 57, GRAND FORKS, NORTH DAKOTA

Stay close to God, because with Him all things are possible. Keep prayer in your life and read inspirational material.

MARION D-H., 51, KNOXVILLE, TENNESSEE

Take care of your future. Love, Grandma

You have finally reached that point in your young life when you answer only to yourself. Sounds wonderful, doesn't it? Or does it feel a little scary? Remember, you have two of the most wonderful resources to turn to for encouragement, help, understanding, and most of all, love: your parents and God. When life gets tough, they will be there for you.

MARY ANN Z., 61, WOODBURY, MINNESOTA

Don't expect the "good life" to be handed to you on a silver platter. Prepare yourself for life by getting a good education. Have goals and do your utmost to achieve them. Don't squander anything—your health, your resources, or the good old common sense you inherited. Don't take any of the above for granted. You can't buy them at any price. They are God's gift to you.

GLADYS S., 88, GRAND FORKS, NORTH DAKOTA

The world you live in is full of opportunities to fulfill your every dream. You will be tempted in many ways, but follow your good common sense and don't be intimidated by anyone.

DOROTHY S., 72, MENOMONIE, WISCONSIN

Decide what you really want to do with your life, then set goals so you can achieve it.

BETTY S., 70, PONCA CITY, OKLAHOMA

Be honest and considerate; it will gain you the trust of others. Without it you have nothing. Money won't buy you happiness—only a few material comforts. Friends, family, and time for yourself should come before work.

SANDRA G., 52, PRINCETON, MINNESOTA

Life is not necessarily meant to be easy, and there is no guarantee that you will be taken care of. Work hard and plan for your future, even into retirement. But set aside some time for fun and relaxation; it makes the rest easier.

JUDY F., 59, WOLCOTT, INDIANA

Be cheerful and friendly to people. Have good work ethics; show up for work and be on time. Don't stand around and gossip, but try to keep busy. Have good people skills and communication skills. Obtain an education that will help you to support yourself. Computer skills are important in this day and age. Do not chew gum at work.

AGNES S., 84, CAVALIER, NORTH DAKOTA

Hold on to your dreams. If you believe you can do it, you will. Set goals and take a step toward them each day.

MARION D-H., 51, KNOXVILLE, TENNESSEE

You can't have everything overnight. Work diligently and you will begin to see the rewards.

S. JEANETTE F., 69, GRAND FORKS, NORTH DAKOTA

Never say "never." We have no idea what the future holds for us.

ETHEL S., 75,
WOODBURY, CONNECTICUT

Life is the happiest and the most worthwhile if you savor planting the seeds, watching them grow, and nurturing them, not just picking the fruit and the flowers.

BARBARA M., 65, MOUND, MINNESOTA

When we were children, we were so eager for life to move along quickly. Go slowly. Everything happens in its time. Life should not be fleeting. It should be slow, rich, and ideally, long.

KATHIE J., 50, LITTLE CANADA, MINNESOTA

Never waver in your pursuits. Reach for the stars; many things are possible. The road of life brings many unexpected twists and turns. It is at these times that you must not swerve. Perhaps around the bend the road of life will again become straight.

FRANCES R., 89, HOLYOKE, MASSACHUSETTS

You are a very special person. Use your God-given talents, and remember that, no matter your age, your grandparents will be there for you.

LOIS W., 59, COLUMBUS, WISCONSIN

Be true to yourself and the principles you have been taught. You are a reflection of the people who have loved and raised you.

KARLEEN P., 57, HUDSON, WISCONSIN

When you fall for any reason, pick yourself up and start anew; after setbacks, you can go forward to a better existence. Keep on learning, which is the key to success.

PATRICIA N., 53, FRIDLEY, MINNESOTA

Be happy when someone else wins the race, the game, the money.

CATHY C., 54, MINNETONKA, MINNESOTA

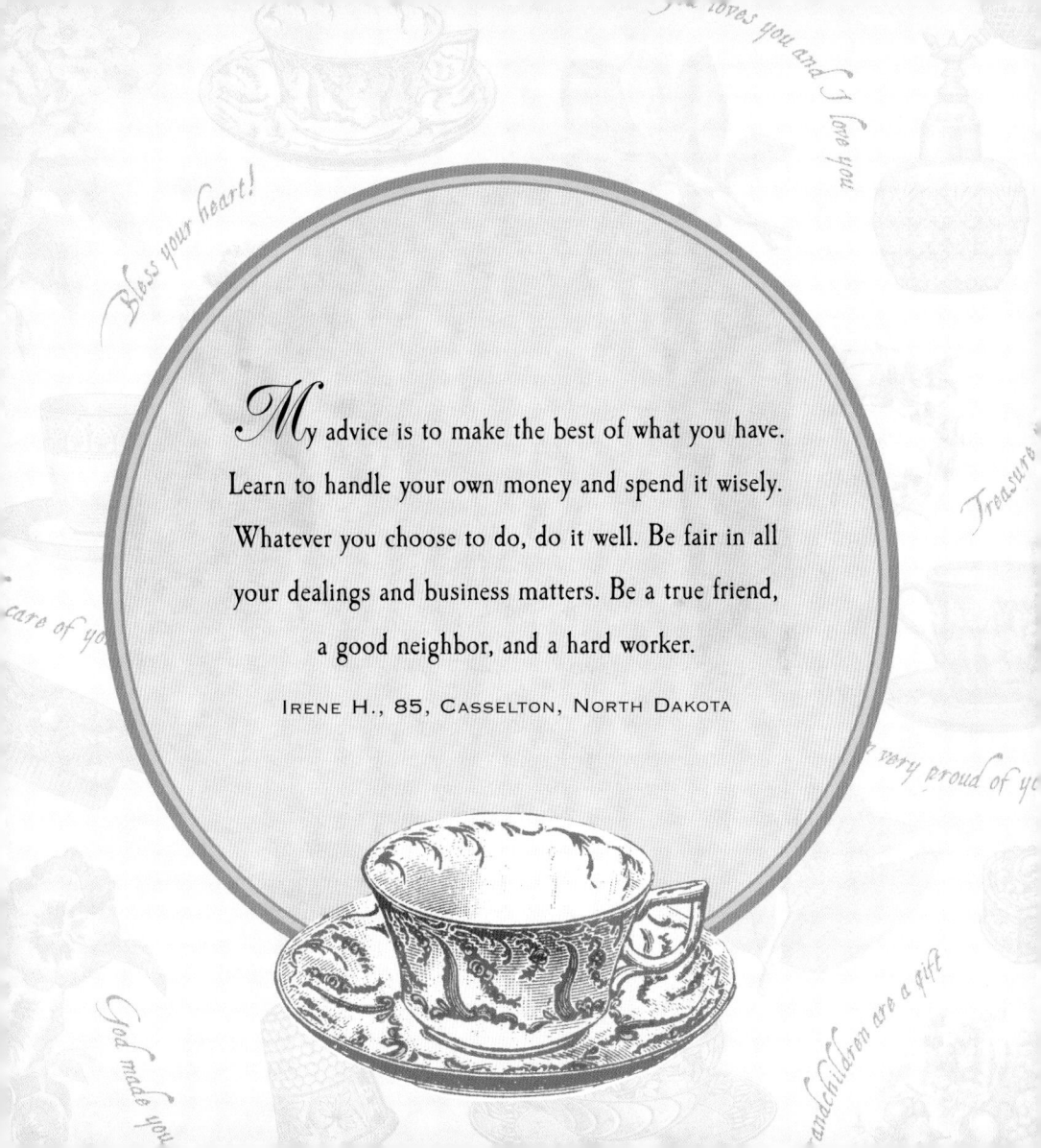

My advice is to make the best of what you have. Learn to handle your own money and spend it wisely. Whatever you choose to do, do it well. Be fair in all your dealings and business matters. Be a true friend, a good neighbor, and a hard worker.

IRENE H., 85, CASSELTON, NORTH DAKOTA

You need short-term and long-term goals in your career, in your personal life, and in your spiritual life. Remember, your goals are yours alone, and only you can achieve them! If you miss your target, don't be discouraged. Bounce back! Re-evaluate, reorganize, and proceed!

JAN A., 59, PRESCOTT, ARIZONA

Know your craft and do it better than the others.

GERALDINE H., 79, KANSAS CITY, MISSOURI

Be clear about who you are and why you are here. Have fun every day. Learn from everything you do. Ask plenty of questions.

BETSY B., 48, DULUTH, MINNESOTA

Develop a positive attitude and expect to achieve success. Your attitudes are self-fulfilling.

GINGER J., 58,
PORTLAND, NORTH DAKOTA

Always save a percent of your income regardless of how small the amount may be. Tomorrow always comes; the sun keeps rising and setting.

FLO E., 56, BISMARCK, NORTH DAKOTA

Take care of your values and beliefs.
Love, Grandma

Family and friends are all-important. As you make choices today, consider how they will affect you tomorrow. Be true to your values.

JEAN V., 71, BALDWIN, WISCONSIN

Values are hard to keep in perspective, but to me they make our lives what they are. The words of advice that top my list are these:

Unselfishness. This is what "earns" love from family and gains you many friends. You can't live without them.

Honesty. When you are one of the oldies you'll not need to regret having hurt someone along the way.

Faith. This is the most important. There is Someone who cares very much about what happens to you.

MARGE B., 74, AUSTIN, MINNESOTA

Examine and define your values. Do not choose to do anything that violates your values. Decisions will come more easily once this framework is in place.

MYRNA N., 56, PLANKINTON, SOUTH DAKOTA

Life is very short. Decide how you want to live it. Set your own direction and go for it!

MARY C., 57, HUDSON, WISCONSIN

Though it is nice to be well thought of and respected, don't compromise your own values and ideas just to gain someone else's acceptance.

SHARON K., 50, CHICAGO, ILLINOIS

Place spiritual values above everything.

ELEANOR B., 73, GOLDEN VALLEY, MINNESOTA

Let your conscience be your guide.
Don't allow a friend to talk you into doing
something you know is wrong.
You can say no! Be your own person.

BEATRICE W., 62, COON RAPIDS, MINNESOTA

You can't go wrong with old-fashioned morality
based on the teachings of the Bible.

MARY JANE B., 75, CHICAGO, ILLINOIS

Greet each day as a wonderful new challenge and a precious gift. You won't have time for preoccupation with past negatives.

PAT S., 71, LARGO, FLORIDA

Enduring values are better than pleasure for the moment.

CAROLYN C., 62, CRYSTAL, MINNESOTA

Keep your word at any cost.

PRISCILLA G., 48, CAMARILLO, CALIFORNIA

As much as possible, live by the Golden Rule and the Ten Commandments.

JEWELL K., 82, LYNNFIELD, MASSACHUSETTS

Hold on to your convictions and don't be afraid to stand by them. Don't allow peer pressure to dictate your moves. Love yourself and like your actions.

PAT J., 59, LAKE VIEW, IOWA

Take care of all the rest. Love, Grandma

Share what you have and you will always be happy.
Happiness is not having what you want,
but wanting what you have.

MARIAN M., 70, ROSEVILLE, MINNESOTA

Make use of the abilities God has given you. Enjoy what is beautiful and believe that as you give to the world, so the world will give to you. Here is a saying that I like:

Do more than exist; live. Do more than touch; feel.
Do more than look; observe. Do more than read; absorb.
Do more than hear; listen. Do more than listen; understand.
Do more than think; ponder. Do more than talk; say something.

– *John H. Rhoades*

JANAHN E., 79, NEWMAN GROVE, NEBRASKA

Experience as many new adventures as you can.

KAROL W., 53, EVERETT, WASHINGTON

Do lots of reading. Cultivate a hobby or something to do when you're alone, such as reading. Nourish your spiritual life through books and prayer. Do something fun for exercise and eat healthy foods.

JEANNE C., 74, ST. PAUL, MINNESOTA

Learn to rejoice in the daily ordinary things and occurrences. Stay hope-filled.

MARIE G., 72, LAMBERTON, MINNESOTA

It's not what you have or how much you have, but who you have to share it with.

LORELIE A., 55, HASTINGS, MINNESOTA

Give to the world the best you have and the best will come back to you. Practice honesty, unselfishness, fairness, compassion, integrity, self-discipline, and belief in God.

MARGARET F., 81, MELBOURNE, FLORIDA

Enjoy life and get involved. Be conscious of and responsible for your actions. Stand up for your rights, but also know when to cooperate. Respect and consider the advice of others, especially your parents.

ANN K., 54, WALES, NORTH DAKOTA

Try to have a garden wherever you live, even if it's a pot on the front step. Plants are good for you and it's good to get your hands dirty now and then. Have fun. The kind of fun that makes you feel good. Clean fun, like a really good game of golf. Get a dog. You'll always have someone to come home to that really wants to see you. Find a friend, a real friend you can confide in. You won't need a psychiatrist. (The dog will help too.) When you look for the love of your life, don't look so much at the outside. Look with your heart, and when you marry, do so with the idea that you're doing this for life. Care about others. Laugh a lot.

JUDY R., 48, BRECKENRIDGE, MINNESOTA

I believe that life is an exciting adventure.
There are valleys and peaks and we must have a zest
for life, a positive attitude, and faith in God.

KAREN W., 48, DETROIT, MICHIGAN

Always wear clean underwear in case
you're in an accident.

FLORENCE B., 82, RHINELANDER, WISCONSIN

You will only have one lifetime.
Fill it full of good memories!

BETTY B., 79, SUN CITY, ARIZONA

Love Grandma

Love Grandma

Love Grandma

Love Grandma